# Passionate Spirituality

*Living And Loving
God's Message*

## John T. Collins

CSS Publishing Company, Inc., Lima, Ohio

PASSIONATE SPIRITUALITY

**Library of Congress Cataloging-in-Publication Data**

Collins, John T., 1973-
    Passionate spirituality : living and loving God's message / John T. Collins.
        p. cm.
    Includes bibliographical references.
    ISBN 0-7880-2602-2 (perfect bound : alk. paper)
    1. Spirituality. 2. Spiritual life—Christianity. 3. Christian life. I. Title.

BV4501.3.C647 2009
248.4—dc22

                                                                    2008032894

For more information about CSS Publishing Company resources, visit our website at
www.csspub.com or email us at csr@csspub.com or call (800) 241-4056.

ISBN-13: 978-0-7880-2606-5
ISBN-10: 0-7880-2606-2                                    PRINTED IN USA

*This book is dedicated to*
*my wife, Nora,*
*for her never-ending*
*love and support.*

# Table Of Contents

# Introduction

How many relationships do you have?

Even if you only have one relationship that you consider to be meaningful you know that it requires you to be a good listener, a generous giver, and most importantly, selfless at times.

Suppose you ignored these qualities in any relationship. What would happen if you never took the time to listen or were never willing to give of yourself? What would happen if you expected the relationship to be all about you? How long do you think this relationship would last? Probably not long!

When relationships are based only on "What I can get from them?" they will eventually disappoint. You probably know that they will lack depth, true intimacy, and of course, sincerity. They might even become a burden. But "give and take" relationships that are mature and healthy can transform lives, bring joy and happiness, and give meaning and purpose to life — depending upon our devotion and commitment.

This is true in the spiritual realm as well. Our relationship with Jesus Christ also requires that we "do something if we expect to have a healthy and meaningful spiritual life." It's been my experience as a pastor and observer that many people rely solely on emotionalism to feed them spiritually (whether it be through contemporary praise music or charismatic preaching). I've learned that those feelings are always fleeting and have no substance when we seek to live a true Christian lifestyle in the face of normal day-to-day stresses and challenges.

Others have become so theologically jaded by "cheap grace" that absolutely no effort is made by the individual believer to grow more Christlike.[1] But we are warned in scripture that "faith without works is dead!" Passionate spirituality is developed when we, with the help of God, desire to change from who we are to whom we are to become. It happens when we make the effort to work with God and capture the vision he has for each one of us and for his church.

So what does a healthy and meaningful spirituality look like? A mature and passionate spiritual life incorporates biblical teachings into daily life. It strives to ever deepen its understanding of God's closeness, wisdom, and grace. It is a daily *practice*, and never a movement toward moral *perfection*. Intentionally awakening your mind to God allows for new insight and increased awareness of the divine's presence. That is what is meant by passionate spirituality in this book and what I hope you find when you begin to examine your faith life anew.

Let me start by saying that this book is not intended to tell you how to awaken your mind, nor is it going to tell you step-by-step what to do to experience a passionate spirituality. This is not a "how to" book. There are plenty of other good books out there that claim they can do that for you.

This book was written to help you discover *where to look* for such a transformation to occur and to show you how Christians with a passionate spirituality practice their faith. It is meant to be a guide that might help you broaden your understanding of what it means to be a spiritual person in the world that we live in and show you that everything you will need to be passionate about your faith is already available to you right under your nose. God has already blessed you. Now it's time that you claim your baptismal identity as a child of God.

I should also point out right from the beginning that I am in no way assuming or implying that one's salvation is dependent upon whether or not they practice what is written in this book. Only God can save his people and bring them into his kingdom. But I can attest to the fact that if you practice these basic principles in all of your affairs you will become more in tune with the working of the Spirit and more in line with what God claimed you were on the day of your baptism. You will be more prepared to see where pruning needs to take place in your daily life and more ready to have that happen with the grace of God. But most importantly, as "you let your light shine before others so that they may see your good works and glorify your Father in heaven" (Matthew 5:16), your praises to the one will be more glorious and sincere than you ever imagined.

In the following chapters we will look at five specific areas of our Christian identity that when cultivated and given proper attention will naturally strengthen our side of the relationship with God here on earth. This has been referred to by some as the five Gs:

- grace
- growth,
- groups,
- giftedness, and
- good stewardship.

Together we will explore how these key areas are vital for the spiritual transformation of every Christian believer and how they pave the way for increased participation in the life of the church, and ultimately, into the world.

Now some of you might wonder why there is not an emphasis on supporting world missions, evangelism, or other social ministry endeavors. Although those areas of ministry are vital to the life of the church I am distinguishing between the *identity* of a Christian and the *mission* of the church as a whole. There is a difference between the two and each needs to be examined separately. Suffice it to say this book will address the spiritual development and transformation of individuals.

So who is this book written for? It's written for all people, believers and unbelievers, who desire to grow deeper in their walk with Jesus Christ. It is meant for people of all Christian denominations or independent churches (Protestant and Roman Catholic). It is written for the neophyte, as well as for those with an "old-time religion." It is written for those who desire to make a difference in the world and for those who want to find the tools needed to do so. And it is my hope that everyone who reads this book might dare to dream of living a godly life like they have never lived before. All for the glory of God.

Although there have been many inspirations for writing this book one of the most important factors occurred when I was having a simple theological discussion with a non-Christian friend. She explained how she believed there was a difference between being spiritual and being religious. She said, "Religious people are those who fear hell, and spiritual people are those who have been to hell." I wasn't sure I agreed with her argument, but at some point in the discussion this friend of mine asked me to tell her how I practiced my own spirituality. All I can remember is that I was puzzled by that question.

I could say to her that I went to church on Sunday mornings, prayed occasionally (especially when I was in trouble), even fasted once or twice (then again that was really just a vain attempt at dieting), but spirituality wasn't a word I was very familiar with. I knew it had everything to do with God and with religious people, but I wasn't accustomed to being asked that question. I always associated spirituality with Eastern religions or new age movements. In fact, in most Lutheran circles (to which I belong) the word "spirituality" is frowned upon by many scholarly theologians because it is such a loaded and difficult word to define. Some say it is a word that is thrown around too loosely.

So I simply said to my friend, "I don't know! But I'll do my best to get back to you."

It's been eight years since I first started wrestling with that question and many influences along the way have helped me put pieces of the puzzle together. There have been many inspirations along the way who have helped develop the ideas found in this book: missiologist and seminary professor, Dr. Richard Bliese, who served at the Lutheran School of Theology at Chicago; the Reverend Susan Swanson and the people of Luther Memorial Church of Chicago; the people of Faith Lutheran Church in Lavallette, New Jersey; the Church of Joy in Arizona; Bill Hybels of Willow Creek Community Church (one of the first ministries to develop the five Gs of Christian identity); Rick Warren of Saddleback Community Church in California; and the Reverend Bruce T. Ewen of the New Jersey Synod (ELCA). I've even had inspiring, and very interesting conversations with people who work a twelve-step program. This book is a collection of some of those conversations and the result of many hours of quiet meditation on the subject.

At places in this book, names have been changed to protect and honor the confidentiality of those who have shared their life stories with me. I thank them for their willingness to be honest, but most importantly, I thank them for including me in their lives.

I suggest, if possible, that you read this book with a group and discuss the content as it pertains to your lives and to your ministry. It's my dearest and deepest desire that you may be blessed by the Spirit as you read this book just as I have been blessed in writing it. May this be the dawning of a new and passionate you!

Much peace!

— John T. Collins

# Chapter One

# Celebrating God's *Grace*

*Therefore, since we are justified by faith, we have peace with God through our Lord Jesus Christ, through whom we have obtained access to this grace in which we stand.* — Romans 5:1

Paul Tillich, one of the twentieth century's finest theologians, once tried to capture the beauty and splendor of God's grace in a series of now-famous sermons and journal articles. He wrote:

*Grace strikes us when we are in great pain and restlessness, when we feel that our separation is deeper than usual, when our disgust for our own being, our indifference, our weakness, our hostility and our lack of direction and composure have become intolerable to us. When, year after year, the longed-for perfection of life does not appear, when the compulsions reign within us as they have for decades, when despair destroys all joy and courage. Sometimes at that moment a wave of light breaks into our darkness, and it is as though a voice were saying: "You are accepted. You are accepted, accepted by that which is greater than you." We may not be better than before, we may not believe more than before. But everything is transformed and nothing is demanded of this experience ... nothing but acceptance.[2]*

Perhaps you've found yourself in great pain and restlessness at some point in your life. Maybe it was like wandering through a wilderness place for longer than you thought you could withstand. Or maybe you're there now. Wherever you find yourself today I'd like to share with you a story about a man named Tom.

Tom's story started in a little Episcopalian church somewhere in New Jersey.[3] He was baptized as an infant, attended Sunday school classes where he first heard the gospel message of Jesus Christ's love for the world, and made his confirmation when he was still in middle school. From the surface, he was a rather ordinary child.

But his life in high school would become anything but ordinary. He recalls that at his very first party, where friends from his school partied in the woods into the wee hours of the night, he got so drunk that he couldn't remember the next day how he had gotten home. In fact, to make matters worse, his entire high school experience would become one big blur.

From high school, Tom went on to experiment with drugs. He worked odd jobs so that he could support his habit and when he was questioned by his parents about his slothful behavior, he'd make up grand stories about one day going back to school to study art and music.

That day never came. The only picture he had painted of himself was that of an addicted, desperate young man who had lost himself along the way. For Tom there would be no higher education or opportunities for self-advancement. There would only be courtrooms, jail cells, and various hospitals to treat his mental and physical pain. For Tom, it was like wandering in a wilderness place with no direction home.

Many wondered what had happened to the young boy whom everyone loved. What happened to the boy who came to church every Sunday and listened to the priest deliver the gospel message of God's amazing grace?

One morning, after a three-day run with cocaine, Tom woke up early in a cheap motel room on the other side of town. He slowly got out of bed, rubbed his eyes, and went over to the window to see what time of the day it was. He opened the shades just enough to let a glimmer of light into the room, and for whatever reason, the beauty of a new day touched Tom in the deepest part of his spirit, giving him a momentary taste of peace and serenity.

He just stood there, he said, thinking about where his life had taken him and wanting more than anything else to end the craziness. So he did what he hadn't done in years — he prayed! He prayed that God would lift the obsession of doing drugs and replace it with peace and serenity. Somewhere in that motel room, clutching onto the shades as if they were a life preserver in rough seas, Tom experienced God's amazing grace.

They say that everyone has a story and today Tom continues to live out his own. He is the man who comes up to receive Communion every Sunday with tears in his eyes thanking Jesus Christ for delivering him from the clutches of hell. He's the one who will belt out songs like it's nobody's business (even though he couldn't carry a tune if his life depended on it). He is even found most Sunday mornings helping to put the chairs away after coffee hour. He's the one who shows compassion for those still struggling to live with an addiction.

I chose to tell Tom's story because it is such a beautiful example of how God can change someone's life for the better. Yes, he had traveled a road that none of us in our right mind would want to travel. Yes, he was lost and found his way back home. Yes, he's now a pleasure to talk with and an inspiration to the people around him. But what makes Tom so special in my mind is that somewhere on his journey he came to understand, and most importantly, *accept* God's grace.

On any given Sunday Tom will tell you that worship is all about celebrating that gift.

### The Way We Celebrate

Christians have such a rich tradition when it comes to their worship. I, for one, love the music and listening to preachers belt out God's word with conviction. I love watching a baptism and receiving communion. I love the elements of mystery that permeate our faith. I love the way liturgy can become like a dance movement when it's done well. I love the drama and the unexpected epiphany moments that remind us of who we are and whose we are. Most of all I love to see people who are passionate about God's amazing grace.

What comes to mind when you think about people who are passionate about God's grace? Perhaps for some it will be the image of a neighbor who recently joined the charismatic church down the road who can't stop telling you what you should or should not do if you want to be saved. If so, there's nothing wrong with that image or that person.

Maybe you think about the man who stands on the street corner with a microphone in one hand and a Bible in the other hand — shouting about the end times and the wrath of God's judgment on the world. Theology aside for a moment, I think that image is fine, as well. I mean, let's face it, you have to be pretty passionate if you're going to stand on a street corner all day.

Perhaps the image of a saint is conjured up or a martyr who died for what she believed. These are all good examples of what passionate, spiritual people look like. Let me see if I can give you another example, one that is oftentimes overlooked and undervalued in the church today.

Years ago, I knew a woman named Eileen whose daughter committed suicide in the basement of their home. Needless to say, this tragedy scarred Eileen in ways I can only imagine. She was a quiet, rather gentle kind of a person who always put the needs of others before her own. She was also the "volunteer" secretary of her church.

From first glance, Eileen fits the mold of most Christians we see. She is reserved, humble as opposed to bold in her proclamation of faith, and fairly quiet when it comes to giving her testimony. She prefers to remain low-key and under the radar screen, rather than be the center of attention.

But what many don't know about Eileen is that she is also one of the most committed people in her church. Whenever the church boiler breaks down, Eileen sends in an anonymous gift to fix it. If the church ladies are baking cookies or pies for a special occasion, Eileen will bake ten times what was asked of her. She sends cards to the shut-ins not because she has to, but because that's the person she has become. And everyone who knows her — loves her.

In some ways she has taken Saint Francis of Assisi's words to heart: "Every where you go preach the gospel message, and if necessary use words!"

She does all of this because somewhere along the way she found God's love in the church she's been a part of for as long as anyone can remember. It was there that a community of friends helped her get through the death of her daughter, and each day of the week she finds her own *authentic* way to celebrate God's amazing grace and give back to the people she loves. Eileen, in her own special way, is as passionate as a Christian can be because her celebration comes from the heart.

Sometimes we're led to believe that passionate Christians have to be loud and visible. Now I'm not saying that there's anything wrong with those who are, but what I want you to also understand is that being passionate about God's grace can express itself in so many ways. There's not a right way or a wrong way. But the best way to celebrate God's grace is by letting that celebration come from your own heart.

### Celebration From The Heart

They say that everyone has a story. That means *you* also have a wonderful story to tell. Your life has been at times exciting and beautiful and perhaps lonely, depressing, or downright frightening. Somewhere along the way, because you are a spiritual being, I want to guess that you've had your own encounter with the Lord. At some point you've stood in awe or felt relieved that a burden was removed. Perhaps, like Job you wrestled with God to find acceptance.

Wherever your faith has taken you I want you to take a moment to think about your own story. Where has the risen Christ been visible in your life? When did you come to understand and appreciate that your past is forgiven and your whole being is deeply loved by God? What feelings arise as you read Deuteronomy 7:6, which says, "For you are a people holy to the Lord your God; the Lord your God has chosen you out of all the peoples on earth to be his people, his treasured possession"?

Christians who celebrate God's grace with a passionate spirituality are always seeking to answer those questions. They come to a worshiping community bringing with them their own story by weaving it together with their faith. It's their own personal experiences that are deeply rooted in their hearts. Why? Because they've lived it and witnessed it, but most importantly, they've embraced it.

What part of your own story can you embrace? Have you been overlooking or ignoring the turning points of your faith life? Do you take too lightly the presence of Christ in your daily affairs?

Perhaps for some it is as simple as growing in a deeper appreciation of your baptism, of table fellowship on Sunday morning, or the blessings you received in hearing your pastor preach a sermon. Maybe you've experienced God's grace as you went through a divorce or after the death of a loved one. Take the time to embrace your story, whatever it may be, and believe that it is unique. Because by embracing it, and seeing that God is working in you on a very personal level, you'll be more likely to want to passionately celebrate God's amazing grace on a daily basis.

## Celebration In All Of Our Affairs

Saint Paul was a man that most people of his day respected. At least, that is to say, if they were Christians and striving to become as passionate as he was in their faith lives. His letters were not only read to the churches they were addressed to, and were considered to be inspired by the Holy Spirit, but they were also treasured as scripture throughout the centuries. To this day, churches around the world read his letters with the utmost respect and admiration.

Here's something encouraging for you and me to think about: Saint Paul never claimed to reach a level of perfection. He always saw himself as he actually was — as broken and in need of a Savior. It was this level of rigorous honesty that allowed him to write this in Romans 7:15: "I do not understand my own actions. For I do not do what I want, but I do the very thing I hate." And then he writes further on in verse 24: "Wretched man that I am! Who will rescue me from this body of death? Thanks be to God through Jesus Christ our Lord!"

You see, being passionate about celebrating God's amazing grace doesn't mean that we have to first become perfect. In fact, what we learn from Saint Paul is that the more he recognized his own shortcomings, the more he grew to appreciate God's gift of forgiveness, redemption, and renewal.

Someone once told me that the most spiritual thing a person can do is to first recognize that they are a sinner. That might sound overwhelming to some of us, but what it means is that only by first recognizing that we have fallen short of God's glory we are then in a position to see that we even need a Savior at all. It requires rigorous honesty about who we are and what we've done, but in doing so it opens the door to a greater appreciation of what Christ has done for us.

Passionate Christians are humble not by nature, but by reflecting daily on the truth. The truth says that we are not deserving of God's grace, nor have we earned it. Nor could we ever earn it. Instead, Christians with a passionate spirituality realize that it is a beautiful gift granted to us. A gift so great that the very salvation of our spirit depends upon it. The promise of everlasting life for all who believe!

This thought might seem foreign to the non-Christian, but this message is central to the faith life of a Christian. It's the reason we can daily celebrate and actually get excited. In fact, 1 Corinthians 1:18 says, "For the message about the cross is foolishness to those who are perishing, but to us who are being saved it is the power of God."

Christians with a passionate spirituality look for ways to show their thanksgiving to Jesus Christ in all of their affairs. Whether it be by following our Lord's call to love our neighbor, or by getting on our knees and praising him for his mercy and his love. It's the power of God working through them and through the people we meet that makes every day a new reason to celebrate and give God our best.

**Bringing Celebration Back Into The Church**
In many ways I was inspired to write this book because I believe that too many churches have forgotten to celebrate God's amazing grace in ways that capture the essence of the gospel message. In other words, Christians are people granted

good news of God's forgiveness and love, and yet when we look out to see the faces of people in our congregations, so often we see anything but excitement. Too often churches become routine, predictable, and shall we say it? Boring!

I'm wise enough to realize that there are many reasons why this may seem true. Perhaps we could blame the pastors for being out of touch. Maybe it's the music director who keeps playing the same old hymns week after week. If you're the pastor you might even be tempted to blame the whole congregation for being boring and unexcitable people by nature. Let's face it, if we wanted to find out who was to blame we could all come up with a long list of names.

Have you ever stopped to think that maybe *you're* the one who is boring? Ouch! I know that might have blindsided you but think about it for a moment. Is there any truth to that statement? Could you be the one who is boring at church?

Now, of course, no one likes to admit that they're boring. I understand that and so do you, but let's go back to what we first said about rigorous honesty. It means that sometimes we have to take a good, solid look at ourselves and see the truth rather than the imaginary.

What excitement are you bringing to church? Are you one of those people who expect to be entertained on Sunday morning? Do you find yourself looking for mistakes made by those reading the lessons rather than actually focusing on what the text says? Do you sing so low that you can't even hear what you're singing? Have you ever told the newcomer, "Hey, that's my seat!"

It's been my experience in meeting and serving with Christians who practice passionate spirituality that they are keenly aware of what they bring to church on Sunday mornings, and they do so for the glory of God. They are less worried about who is to blame and more focused on their own contribution.

21

I remember meeting Charlie (a man in his late eighties) when I returned to my home parish while I was doing my undergraduate studies. What impressed me the most about Charlie was how energetic and excited he was to be there every Sunday morning. He was an usher and without missing a beat Charlie hugged every single person who walked through that door.

One day I remember asking Charlie why he was always so happy and so excited about Sunday mornings. He simply said, "I'm just doing my part!" That always kind of stuck with me.

Are you doing your part? Do you bring any excitement to church on Sunday or do you just sit there waiting to be moved or entertained?

Let me close with something I have learned from Christians who practice a passionate spirituality: Church will never be boring if you understand and remember that it's not about you. It's about worshiping and praising God for his amazing and awesome grace!

## Time For Reflection

1. Think of a time you experienced God's amazing grace. What happened? What were the emotions that you felt? Who did you share it with? How did it change your life?

2. How do you celebrate God's amazing grace today?

3. What describes God's grace for you?

4. Where do you experience God's amazing grace most?

5. If you could say one thing to God right now for what he has done in your life what would you say? How would you show your appreciation?

# Chapter Two

# The *Growth* Factor

*He said therefore, "What is the kingdom of God
like? And to what should I compare it? It is like a
mustard seed that someone took and sowed in the
garden; it grew and became a tree, and the birds
of the air made nests in its branches." And again
he said, "To what should I compare the kingdom
of God? It is like yeast that a woman took and
mixed in with three measures of flour until all of it
was leavened."*                      — Luke 13:18-21

The Bible tells us that as children of God we are made in
his image. I understand there are many different understand-
ings as to what that means, but what I want to bring to your
attention as you read this chapter is that we are all made to
grow and become more like him. Now I'm not referring to
physical growth. I'm talking about spiritual growth. But in
order to do so we must first prune away those areas of our life
that cause our growth to be hindered. Let me see if I can give
you an example.

Not far from where we live there's a water slide park that
opens every summer. It's not easy to miss because on any
given day in July or August tourists fill the entire park. As
you drive by you see families and teenagers having the time
of their life. But what you'll also notice is that every slide has
a long line of people patiently waiting their turn. That is, with
the exception of one slide that most people fear. I like to call
it "suicide run" and you can be sure there's never anyone in
that line.

I've named it "suicide run" because it stands over fifty feet in the air suddenly dropping straight down into a pool of ice cold water. It's so frightening that rumors have spread throughout the area of people having heart attacks on the way down. I'm not sure they're true stories, but by the look of the slide I could see that being a strong possibility.

I will be the first to admit that I don't like heights, nor do I like thrill rides. One day this particular slide kept calling out my name, almost challenging me to face my fears. Finally, after much consideration, and praying that God would miraculously intervene and close the slide down, I made my way to the top of the slide — ready to face my fears!

As I stood at the very top all I could hear was the whistling of the wind. The people below looked like ants, and the view of the entire shoreline was visible. I felt weak in my knees and my stomach was beginning to fill with those nervous butterflies. I wondered to myself as to whether or not I had lost my mind, but I knew that there was no turning back.

Slowly I sat down on the slide and looked down below. I truly wanted to cry, but before I could get up and leave, something inside of me gave me the courage to let go of the bars and overcome my fear. I landed below in the cold water three seconds later with my bathing suit now fitting like a thong, but also having a great sense of pride within myself. I had faced that which I feared and have discovered that just as in the spiritual realm, each time we do so — we grow to become a new person.

I am fully convinced that one of the biggest stumbling blocks to spiritual growth is fear. So many times we let that which we are afraid of get in the way of serving God. And what we're actually giving up when we allow ourselves to be overcome is the chance to grow into the *passionate Christians* God has called us to become.

Do you remember the story of Moses? One of the first things Moses feared was his lacking eloquence of speech. (Read Exodus 4:10-17.) God chose Moses to lead his people out of Egypt, and to do so he would have to speak before the Pharaoh and the Israelites. Yet, Moses didn't want to go because he was afraid he would fail.

Just imagine if Moses never went....

Do you remember the story of Jesus calling for Simon Peter to follow him? (Read Luke 5:1-11.) The first thing Simon Peter said was, "Go away from me, Lord, for I am a sinful man!" Believing he was unqualified to live up to Jesus' expectations, and afraid he would be rejected, he nearly threw away the chance of a lifetime.

Imagine if Simon Peter didn't find the courage to answer Jesus' call....

You see, fear can dominate our thinking and lead us to believe we're unqualified or unfit to answer God's call to serve him. When we allow this to happen we never grow into the person God wants us to become. But you know what I've discovered along the way? Christians who have a *passionate spirituality* put themselves *out there* even if doing so frightens them at times. They take the time to prune away that which hinders the greatest spiritual growth.

Some of the best preachers I know today were at one point afraid of public speaking. Many singers, who have beautiful voices and a great stage presence, didn't wake up one day feeling comfortable in front of a large crowd. It took time, practice, and courage. I guess I could go on and on with other examples where I've seen this to be true, but what I want you to see is that in order for any Christian to grow *passionate* about their spirituality they must first be willing to take risks and trust that God will never call us to do anything unless he first believes that we can succeed.

In the rest of this chapter I'd like to highlight three areas of our spirituality that if cultivated and given attention, will allow us to grow to become the passionate Christian we all desire to be. These areas include *knowledge*, *prayer*, and *love*.

## Growing In Knowledge

One of my favorite seminary professors would always say, "Faith without works is dead, but faith without knowledge is deadly!" What he meant was that some of the greatest atrocities in human history (such as the Crusades, the Holocaust, and more) have been led by so-called Christians who had some sense of faith in Jesus Christ, but who lacked knowledge in what Jesus actually taught. The end result can often be dangerous, to say the least, and can also misrepresent our faith.

As we read our newspapers and listen to the nightly news we see this to be the case in certain fundamentalist Islamic groups. Although I am not a Muslim, nor confess to be well versed in the Koran, I find it hard to believe that Islam has so successfully survived throughout the centuries because it calls for killing, slander, and intolerance of others. Rather, I believe that ignorance is to blame for the most recent atrocities we've seen done in the name of Islam.

We might even see this in our own local churches today. I heard of one church whose council couldn't get along on any matter. One particular night they were engrossed in a very serious and heated debate over which color the hall carpet should be. Things got so out of hand that the president and the treasurer actually got into a fistfight with each other. Faith without knowledge is deadly!

You see, authentic *spiritual growth* requires not only a deep-seated belief in Jesus Christ, but it also requires constant study and reflection. Would you take a doctor very seriously if he told you that he went to medical school, yet never studied? Or a lawyer who never read her law books? Of course not! So why would it be any different for a Christian? We must also pursue higher levels of understanding when it comes to our faith.

I've heard it said that going to McDonald's doesn't make us a hamburger, any more than going to church makes us a Christian. Christians who practice a passionate spirituality understand that part of growing into the people God would have us become means we continue to study and learn about the teachings of scripture, church doctrine, church history, and other areas, because in doing so we are then in a position to celebrate our faith with integrity.

Why is it that so few people want to do that? I'm sure there are many possible answers to that question, but one of the most common reasons I have heard is that many people are afraid. They are afraid someone is going to see how little they know about the Bible. They are afraid they are going to get nothing out of it. They are afraid they are going to be challenged to change their lifestyles. They are afraid it's going to be too big a commitment. The list could go on and on, but suffice it to say, fear seems to once again be the greatest stumbling block for spiritual growth in our churches today.

Let me give you an example of how I've seen this to be true. A few years ago, I started a Bible study for beginners. There were about ten people in the group and I'll never forget the look of frustration on one woman's face when they were all asked to open their Bibles to the book of Genesis. That poor woman, who had been coming to church for as long as anyone could remember, finally confessed, saying, "Pastor, I can't find it!"

At first I thought she was kidding, but realized after a few moments that she was serious. She had been coming to church for nearly 45 years and couldn't find the first book of the Bible. She later went on to tell me that she was always afraid of being made fun of or looking stupid, which is why she never attended a Bible study before. It wasn't long after she confronted her fear that she started to ask questions.

I always tell the people in the congregation I serve that a good question is always better than a bad answer. I encourage the people around me to question and to wonder about scripture. Because truth be told, none of us have all the answers. None of us have all wisdom. However, by asking questions and striving to find the right answers we can grow in understanding, and what's more, we grow in knowledge of God's word, church doctrine, and church history. All of which help us to grow more passionate in our spirituality.

No one knew this truth better than Martin Luther. Although Martin Luther was a preacher, teacher, scholar, pastor, father, and husband, he always believed that at the core of his faith, study was important. John Piper, reflecting on Luther's life, wrote:

> *For Luther, the importance of study was so interwoven with his discovery of the true Gospel that he could never treat study as anything other than utterly crucial and life-giving and history shaping. Study had been his gateway to the gospel and to the Reformation and to God. We take so much for granted today about truth and about the Word that we can hardly imagine what it cost Luther to break through to the truth, and to sustain access to the Word. Study mattered. His life and the life of the church hung on it. We need to ask whether all the ground gained by Luther and the other Reformers may be lost over time if we lose this passion for study, while assuming that truth will remain obvious and available.*[4]

Some say we are living in an anti-intellectual society. As I understand it we are more focused on entertainment than on education. A good example of this is found when one looks at the yearly income of a schoolteacher against the yearly income of a basketball, football, or baseball player. The problem is that this resistance to learning has also made its way into our churches as well. Would it be too bold to say that the fastest growing churches in America today are the ones that place a heavy emphasis on entertainment and emotionalism rather than on learning and reflection? I'll let you be the judge of that!

A few weeks ago, I was talking to a friend who happens to be a Pentecostal Christian. Although we differ theologically on just about every issue, I love carrying on conversations with her because so often she challenges me to consider things I wouldn't normally think about. That day we were discussing infant baptism and I had prepared numerous scriptural and theological references as to why I believed it was God's will. Finally after a few minutes of discussing this with her she finally said to me, "Pastor, you think too much!"

I think in her own kind way she was trying to tell me that sometimes my faith circulates too heavily in my mind and perhaps not enough in my heart. I've come to believe that authentic faith needs to be fairly balanced. It's not enough to say that we have all faith and yet lack knowledge. Otherwise, we'd be unable to make ethical decisions with integrity. We'd be nothing more than robots. What's worse, we wouldn't be using one of the greatest gifts that God has given to us — our minds.

Let me challenge you to consider growing in your own understanding of what you say you believe. Realize that true spiritual growth requires effort and courage on your part, but as with anything else that is desirous, it leads to a greater sense of passion and commitment along the way. Church shouldn't be a place where we are entertained. Church should be a place where we are challenged to grow into the person God would have us become.

## Growing In Prayer

I always liked the story of the old man who lived in a very corrupt city. Crime was rampant, addiction was epidemic, and very few people knew the Lord. Suffice it to say it wasn't a very hopeful place to live.

Every morning that man got up, went down to the street below, and yelled out at the top of his lungs, "Keep praying to God!"

Afternoon would come and that man would go down again and yell out, "Keep praying to God!"

Again, in the evening, he would go down into the street and yell out, "Keep praying to God!"

The old man didn't make everyone on the block very happy with his constant yelling. In fact, one of the neighbors met the old man in the street one day and said, "Listen, old man, all of your yelling and screaming about praying to God isn't going to change things around here. Don't you know that there's crime and corruption and all sorts of trouble in this city? Why not give it a rest? You're not going to change the world!"

The old man thought about it for a moment and then said, "You know, you're right. My constant screaming about praying to God isn't going to change the world, but one thing's for sure, it's going to keep the world from changing me."

First Thessalonians 5:17 says, "Pray without ceasing." This means that God loves to hear our voices all through the day. God loves to hear what's on our minds and in our hearts. God loves for every one of us to constantly speak to him on a daily basis.

I've found that our prayers often cease when we feel intimidated by what others will think of us. Unlike that old man who wouldn't let the world change him, so many of us do just that. We keep our spiritual life private for none to see and go along with what the world expects from us. Perhaps we do this so as not to push our beliefs on others, nor to offend anyone. How offensive it must seem to God that we'd rather hide him than make him known through our confidence in prayer. What's worse? We miss the opportunity to hear God speak to us!

I've always been attentive to the text in Luke 9:26 that says, "Those who are ashamed of me and of my words, of them the Son of Man will be ashamed when he comes in his glory and the glory of the Father and of the holy angels." Do we not pray openly without ceasing because we are ashamed of Jesus Christ? I don't have the answer to that question, but as you think about where you are in your own prayer life ask yourself if there's any truth in it for you.

This chapter is not a manual on how to pray or what to pray. There are plenty of books already written on that subject. I believe you already know how to pray. There's a way that feels comfortable and natural for you. It might be that you enjoy praying written prayers, or repeating mantra prayers, or the Lord's Prayer. Maybe you're one of those people who prefers spontaneous prayer. However it is that you feel most comfortable praying, all I'd like to suggest is that you do so with perseverance and without ceasing on a daily basis. Then, here's the key to effective prayer — we must listen!

When we read the gospels we will often find Jesus praying alone. He made it a priority every single day to center himself in prayer. I'd like to believe that he did this not only to give the Father thanksgiving and blessing, but so that he could constantly discover the Father's will by listening to him.

In fact, some of the Christians that I know who have a *passionate spirituality* will tell me that they never make an important decision without first praying. Whenever they need direction or focus, prayer becomes the center of their lives. Their prayers are not focused on getting something as much

33

as they are focused on getting closer to God by listening to what he will reveal.

Begin to practice these same principles in your own life. Realize that at first, daily prayer may seem difficult, uncomfortable, or even challenging for you to stay focused. You might even have a hard time hearing God's voice at first. But through time you will be better able to discern God's will for your life, and not only will you grow more comfortable in speaking openly to your creator, you'll begin to hear his voice. Go ahead, see if what I'm saying is true! Before reading any further, why not say a prayer?

**Growing In Love**

One of the observations I've made, after meeting many different Christian people along the way, is that oftentimes I find there can be an imbalance in one's spirituality. So often we find that someone has plenty of intellectual knowledge of God, and yet lacks an active prayer life. Or there are those who love to pray long prayers, and yet live with nothing more than a Sunday school understanding of their faith. Finally, what I find more often are those who are very well educated when it comes to understanding their faith and know how to pray eloquent prayers, yet lack the last most important part of their faith development — love.

Some people say God spoke more about money than any other subject. I think that statement is wrong. Jesus spoke more about love than any other subject. Love is at the very heart of our gospels and our faith. Without love, the Bible says, we are nothing. (Read 1 Corinthians 13.) Jesus spoke of the greatest commandment.

> *"Hear, O Israel: the Lord our God, the Lord is one; you shall love the Lord your God with all your heart, and with all your soul, and with all*

*your mind, and all your strength." The second is
this, "You shall love your neighbor as yourself."
There is no greater commandment greater than
these.* — Mark 12:29-31

What Jesus is telling us is that authentic *passionate spiri-tuality* must include love. Seems simple enough. But if we read Jesus' words carefully we see that this commandment requires every ounce of our being. It is not to be approached haphazardly or lightly, but with great effort and determination. It's been my experience that love, at least true love, is not easily practiced because it calls for all of us to be giving of our time, honest in all matters, and always considerate to all people around us. It means that we allow ourselves to be vulnerable.

Here's what I want you to consider: Jesus is asking us to grow in three areas — love of neighbor, love of God, and love of self. How do we do that?

Rather than give an answer, let me see if I can suggest where the journey can begin. Think back to what was said in chapter 1: Appreciating God's grace begins when we come to terms with our own true nature. By doing that, we come to see that we are flawed and have made our own mistakes. In fact, it would be arrogant for us to believe that we are better than anyone else. When we're rigorously honest about our own shortcomings, weaknesses, and failures we are then in a position to have compassion for the people around us. Jesus once said, "Why do you see the speck in your neighbor's eye, but do not notice the log in your own eye?" (Luke 6:41).

I've also always been challenged by what it says in 1 John 4:20: "Those who say, 'I love God,' and hate their brothers or sisters are liars; for those who do not love a brother or sister whom they have seen, cannot love God whom they have not seen." Yikes!

35

You know, we can look around and see ugliness in the eyes of our neighbors. We can get focused on how poor a person's character is, and if we really get focused on all the negative qualities of these people we can begin to hate them. As spiritual people we must understand that just like a child who can have unexplainable love for a rag doll God loves all of his people much the same way, and to want to destroy or hurt something that means so much to God only hurts our relationship with him as well.

We're called to love people in this world (just as God loved us even when we were caught up in sin). We're called to see the people around us as brothers and sisters, and in the process we're called to become more like Christ himself. It's not easy to do, but it's the very purpose of our faith.

Every once in while we meet people who share this same vision. We meet people who are compassionate, caring, and faithful. They accept you for who you are whether good or bad, and I can bet that if you've ever met such a person in your own life you've probably never forgotten them. Because these are the people that have seen you the way that God sees you — broken, yet lovable.

I'll never forget my second grade Sunday school teacher. She probably stood five feet tall, had long, brown hair, a cute little smile, and had one of the nicest personalities I can re-member. I always thought when I was in her class that she had been sent to us by God. In my active imagination I thought of her as an angel. She was caring and compassionate and always had kind things to say.

One Sunday, a little boy named Michael had joined our class. He was a year older than all of us, but looked younger because he was very thin and frail looking. His hair (even at that young age) was seemingly gray and missing patches. He wasn't very tall, nor did he have a lot to say. I found out years later that he had a rare form of leukemia that had stunted his growth.

I can remember how on that first day some of the children in the class started picking on him and calling him names. One child started spitting spitballs on him, and just as tears began to fall from Michael's eyes, the teacher saw what was going on.

Immediately, she stopped what she was doing, went over to little Michael, and put her arms around his neck. Then I'll never forget what she said to our class. She said, "Is this how you're going to live the rest of your lives? Teasing and hurting people who God loves?" And from that day on, no one in the class ever teased Michael again.

I guess in some ways I've spent most of my life up to this point trying to answer that question. What kind of a person will I be known as when I die? A person filled with anger, hatred, and prejudice? Or will I be known as a child of God who loves, cares, and has compassion for others?

Maybe a better question to ask is, "What will people remember about you?"

I've learned something from Christians who practice a passionate spirituality that loving is a one-day-at-a-time venture. Each day, they remind themselves that sometimes God calls them to hold hands with those who sit in darkness. Sometimes they are called to give of themselves. Sometimes to be patient. Sometimes they're called to resist taking offense with people who are spiritually sick.

To love people the way that God loves us is difficult — but when we strive to do so we meet the risen Christ again and again along the way. It is my prayer that we Christians around the world grow to become more loving in our hearts, more concerned for the needs of others, but most importantly, that we grow to love the Lord our God with all of our heart, all of our mind, and with all our soul and that we love our neighbors as we love ourselves. Because it's in doing these things that our faith becomes our passion.

## Time For Reflection

1. What area of your spiritual life needs the most growth? (Examples may include Bible study, learning about church history or doctrinal theology, and getting involved.)

2. Where have you seen the greatest growth within yourself? How were you able to grow?

3. What style of prayer works best for you? At what point during the day do you pray? What do you find yourself praying for the most?

4. How do you share Christ's love in the world? Where would you like to start sharing God's love?

5. Tell of a time you were able to overcome a fear and share how it changed your life.

# Chapter Three

# *Groups:* Friendships, Family, And Fellowship

*All who believed were together and had all things in common; they would sell their possessions and goods and distribute the proceeds to all, as any had need. Day by day, as they spent much time together in the temple, they broke bread at home and ate their food with glad and generous hearts, praising God and having the goodwill of all the people. And day by day the Lord added to their number those who were being saved.*

— Acts 2:44-47

If you are reading this book with a group of people from your church, I have good news for you! You are already practicing one of the most important elements of your spiritual development and doing what the very first group of Christians we read about in the book of Acts did. You are engaging with other Christians and building an inner circle of friends who can potentially become lifelong companions on your own faith journey.

We know from reading our Bibles that even Jesus Christ didn't go it alone. He gathered around him twelve disciples, and then hundreds of other men and women he chose to call "friends" (John 15:15). He did this because God has made all of us to be social creatures. We need the interaction of others so that we might be held accountable and challenged to become better Christians, so that we might have someone to confide in and share our feelings with, so that we might learn from and teach others. But most importantly so that we may love and be loved.

My experience as a minister has shown me that people are more likely to stay connected with a church if they have joined a group and built relationships along the way. They might join a Bible study, a prayer group, or a men's ministry. It might even be something as simple as joining a small group of people making the coffee after worship. Whatever the group may look like, it is those friendships that keep us connected to a house of worship and help us to feel at home.

The saddest thing I see in ministry settings today is people who prefer to sit alone in worship, who are always the first ones to leave, and who never make any effort at meeting other Christian men and women in their church. It saddens me because I don't think they know how wonderfully healthy and holistic small groups can be. I don't think they know how awesome it is when someone other than the pastor says, "I prayed for you this morning. How are you doing?" Or, "If you need to talk I'm here for you."

Being part of a group in your church can be life-changing and life-giving. It takes away the fear that we will ever be doing ministry alone or without company, which is why God has blessed the church with the gift of community and given to all of us the opportunity to belong. It's what makes the church so special.

In her most recent book, Kelly A. Fryer wonders if it's even possible to be the church if there's no fellowship or camaraderie. She wrote:

> *From the very beginning, there has been an important connection between being the church* **out there** *and coming together,* **in here***. There was something about being the church out on the street that made people want to share a life together,* **in here***. There was something about being the church*

*in the world that made them want to eat and pray and study God's Word together and share their stories. But this is also true: there had to have been something about the way those people came together **in here** — something about the way they prayed and worshipped and shared their stories and learned and laughed together — that made it possible for them to be the church **out there**.*[5]

I would agree that fellowship is the backbone of the church. It's what keeps us strong, fresh, and vital. Most importantly it's what makes the mission of the church possible for our generation and the next.

## Why Do We Keep Looking For More?

I always liked the story about the woman named Mary who would always make frequent trips to the post office. One day she was confronted with a very long line of people waiting for service from the clerks. One observer discovered that Mary only needed a few stamps and asked, "Why don't you use the stamp machine? You can get all the stamps you need there and you won't have to stand in line." Mary said, "I know, but the machine can't ask me about my arthritis."

Just take a look around the world today and you'll find people just like Mary who seek love, caring, or acceptance and yet seek it in all the wrong places. They may look for it in a bar, online in chat rooms or dating services, or perhaps in extreme cases — at the post office. So many people go to great extents to find what already exists in the church today. Yet, they don't even know that it is there. What I've found to be particularly alarming is that this is true for Christians already attending a church as well. Sometimes even Christians don't know where to find authentic, meaningful faith-based relationships.

Just the other day I was speaking with an inactive member of my own church. I wondered why she never gets more involved in the fellowship aspects of our church. She looked at me and said, "I have plenty of friends outside of the church. I am not lonely like some of these people."

I knew in my heart she had no idea what she was missing because the kind of fellowship one finds in a Christian group is unlike anything you'll find outside of the church.

In fact, Dietrich Bonhoeffer once remarked,

> *Christian brotherhood is not an ideal which we must realize; it is rather a reality created by God in Christ in which we may participate. The more clearly we learn to recognize that the ground and the strength and promise of all our fellowship is in Jesus Christ alone, the more serenely shall we think of our fellowship and pray and hope for it.*[6]

If you're one of the people who avoids belonging to a Christian group, ask yourself these questions: "What do people outside of the church know about your faith, your ethics, or your hope in Jesus Christ? How many deep-seated spiritual conversations can you carry on with friends who don't know the Lord or who don't practice their faith like you do? How can an outsider help or lead you to grow spiritually?"

We Christians have our own language, our own traditions, and our own way of living that seems foreign to the rest of the world, but thanks be to God, it is our identity. It is in biblically based Christian small groups where we find our greatest element of connectedness and spiritual familiarity. It's where true fellowship exists and blossoms.

Saint Paul once wrote these words to the Corinthian church (who also struggled with some of the same issues):

*Do not be mismatched with unbelievers. For what partnership is there between righteousness and lawlessness? Or what fellowship is there between light and darkness? What agreement does Christ have with Beliar? Or what does a believer share with an unbeliever? What agreement has the temple of God with idols? For we are the temple of the living God; as God said, "I will live in them and walk among them, and I will be their God, and they shall be my people. Therefore come out from them, and be separate from them, says the Lord, and touch nothing unclean; then I will welcome you, and I will be your father, and you shall be my sons and daughters, says the Lord Almighty."* — 2 Corinthians 6:14-18

If you are involved in a worshiping community of believers, you have been given a very special and unique opportunity. You have been given an opportunity to live with and among people who love God as much as you do. That opportunity is found when you seek belonging to a small group within your church.

I want to show you how belonging to a group can help you to grow more passionate about your own spirituality. First, by belonging to a group *we get to know each other better*. By belonging to a group *we get to know ourselves better*. Finally, by belonging to a group *we get to know Jesus Christ better*.

## We Get To Know Each Other Better

Bob joined our Bible study somewhere in the early part of the spring. He arrived that day unexpectedly carrying a Bible in one hand and a biblical commentary in the other. He wasn't a member of our church but was known around town by a few. He was a rather quiet man who always wore a frown

43

on his face and rarely did he take the time to make eye contact with anyone. To make matters worse he was hard of hearing, and when he finally did answer you he would do so with an aggravated, annoyed tone. He seemed rude, arrogant, and emotionless. All who knew of him walked on pins and needles around him. All others just avoided him at all costs. One couldn't help but wonder what had made this man so miserable.

That spring, we were studying the gospel of Mark and to everyone's surprise Bob had come for three weeks in a row. He would quietly sit at the end of the table, looking down at his notes, while the group discussed the text. That day we were discussing the story of Jairus' daughter being raised from the dead (Mark 5:21-43) when suddenly Bob piped up for the first time, saying, "My daughter wasn't that lucky!"

We all just froze. It was as if a great sage had finally spoken after years of silence. No one dared to make a noise or interrupt. We just sat there wondering if Bob would say anything more. Finally, after taking off his glasses and rubbing his eyes, Bob shared how his daughter had died when she was only seventeen years old. He told us about the pain he had been carrying for years and how he had prayed that God should have taken him and not his daughter. He expressed anger, guilt, and sadness. It took every ounce of our beings not to cry as Bob spoke.

Bob kept coming week after week from that point on. In fact, the participants in the group grew to like him and would now speak to him and ask him how he was doing. In time, Bob shared more of what he believed about God (and how the world works), and he became a very important person to all of us. Then, as quickly as Bob had arrived, Bob stopped coming. Some of us tried calling, others rang the bell on his Southside Chicago apartment, but none of us could get in touch with him. That next week we learned that Bob had died in his sleep.

I can tell you that Bob was greatly missed after he had died. It seemed to many of us that something was missing from the group. Ironically, the man who seemed so unfriendly and crabby at first had become a friend to all of us. Not only that, his vulnerability and courage in sharing his pain helped the group to become more sincere in their own sharing. It was as if we were given permission to open up. It was an important turning point for the group. We were, in our own way, becoming more like Bob.

This is one of the things that I see lacking in many churches. So often when we see each other in casual settings we never really tell the whole truth. Everyone seems like they're trying to "fake it until they make it." Someone may ask us, "How are you doing?" Our response often is, "Fine!" But many times we are not fine. Perhaps there is trouble at home or with our children or at our job. We know that in casual settings it is not the right time to share all that is going in our life. We believe that deep down people really don't want to hear everything. We know that the people who are asking how we are doing are just being polite. So we hold it in and put on the mask, hoping to get through the day.

The beautiful thing about a small group is that we don't have to wear masks or be anything other than real. We can be ourselves, and we can get to know what is really going on in each other's lives.

By doing this, so often we discover that we're not the only one having a bad day or even a bad year. By taking the time to listen to one another, and by being heard, we often discover that disappointments, setbacks, or grief are common to everyone. Whenever I hear that someone else is going through what I'm going through, I get a feeling of relief knowing that I'm not alone. Someone else understands my pain —

someone who is Christian and a part of a group where I belong.

To know and to be known seems to capture for me what a beautiful relationship could look like. Being able to be honest with people and still be accepted is what we're all looking for, isn't it?

Let the truth be told that all Christians need this support in their own ministry as well. We are created to be social and to interact with others. It's how God designed us and it's what helps us to grow deeper in our spirituality and become more connected to the people we serve. Thanks be to God it can be found in a small group.

A few days after Bob died, a few of us from the Bible study went to the funeral. The saddest thing was that there were only a handful of people present. No one seemed to be overly upset at his passing. No one was crying. It was obvious that Bob had chased away many people in his life. In fact, some present could only remember Bob as the man with the frown. Those of us who had heard his story and felt his pain knew more about the man. We knew about the courage he had in sharing his story. We knew about the pain he struggled with on a daily basis. We knew about the prayers he prayed every single day. Most importantly, we knew that in Bob there was a good man who only wanted to be known and heard.

Isn't that what we're all looking for?

## We Get To Know Ourselves Better

The second gift of belonging to a small group is that we have the opportunity to better know ourselves.

Years ago, when I was in seminary fulfilling a three-month Clinical Pastoral Education program (also known as CPE), I was assigned to a hospital on Long Island, New

York. I visited patients weekly, Monday through Friday. As part of the requirement, we were assigned to a small group to discuss our progress, our feelings, and our thoughts. This group met every day from 1-2 p.m. and would usually tackle a number of topics each week.

On one particular day, about six months into the program, we were encouraged to get in touch with our own feelings. This, we were told, would help us to stay "present" with the patients we met in the hospital and allow us to grow as ministers who could be emotionally present. In my mind, I didn't have much feeling either way. I wasn't saddened by the experience of being in a hospital, nor was I overly thrilled to be there. I guess in some ways I felt emotionless.

That day, our supervisor challenged us to dig deeper. He asked me to tell him what thoughts came to mind when I heard the word "hospital." I remember sitting there for a few moments wondering about his question. Finally I said, "My father's death!"

With that, the images of my father lying in a hospital bed immediately came back to me. The images of the priest holding my hand and telling me that my father was going to be in a better place haunted me. I remember the tears that fell from the eyes of my two sisters as we said good-bye. All of these memories came back to me like the waters of a flood and I started getting restless in my chair, crossing my arms and my legs, as I made the connection between hospitals and my feelings. I hadn't allowed myself to think about it for over five years. I just blocked it out of my mind. Now, there was no place to hide.

Obviously noticing there was more to me than I was allowing the group to see, the supervisor said to me, "Tell me about your father." Before I could get a word out I started to cry bitterly. It was one of those cries that forces the mouth to open and yet remains silent. My pain was no longer within me. It was on show for all to see, as I sobbed like a little child.

What I remember most about that moment was the love that everyone in the group showed me. A few put their arms around me and gave me a hug. Some told me that it was all right to cry. A few even cried themselves. What I'll never forget, as long as I live, is how that group helped me to know myself more. I had no idea that I was holding back so much pain. I had no idea that hospitals were so emotionally painful for me. I tried to block it all out and keep my emotions bottled up. But with the help of that group I was able to dig deeper into myself and identify the truth of who I was. In doing that they gave me a true gift, one that I've taken with me wherever the Lord will have me go.

How well do you know yourself? I want to guess that you probably don't know yourself as well as you think you do. Ultimately, getting to know yourself better is up to you and God has given you a chance to do so. But no one can force you to do it. You can remain where you are today, or you can get involved in a small group that will help you to become an even better person today and accept you along the way. You can know and be known on a much deeper level than you ever imagined. You can know about the love that is only found in a group of Christians like yourself. But as with all things it's up to you.

## We Get To Know Jesus Christ Better

Jesus once said, "For where two or three are gathered in my name, I am there among them" (Matthew 18:20).

It has been my experience that when we belong to a small group we also learn to know Jesus Christ in entirely new ways. We begin to see Jesus in others and sometimes in ourselves. This happens because so often God will send someone who is in need of help to a group of Christians. God may send to

48

the group a person new to the faith, or someone who is mentally or physically sick, or someone who is financially needy or without food and shelter. He may even send someone who is simply in need of a listening ear. Each time we find these people, God calls us to minister to them.

Jesus once said,

> *Then the righteous will answer him, "Lord, when was it that we saw you hungry and gave you food, or thirsty and gave you something to drink? And when was it that we saw you a stranger and welcomed you, or naked and gave you clothing? And when was it that we saw you sick or in prison and visited you?" And the king will answer them, "Truly I tell you, just as you did it to one of the least of these who are members of my family, you did it to me."* — Matthew 25:37

God calls us to take care of the most vulnerable of society and commands that we share whatever resources we have available. He calls us to give of our time, our talent, and treasures freely. It's in the doing of these things that we not only become more like Christ himself, but we learn firsthand what the Christian life is all about. It's about service to others and being part of a fellowship that will give us endless opportunities to serve the Lord.

A few years ago, friends of mine brought their former housekeeper to our group. She was an older African-American woman who had the heart of a saint. During the evening we got to know her and enjoyed her company very much. At the end of the night, after we had finished putting the chairs and tables away, she revealed to some of us that her son was in prison. You could just tell that this broke her heart. Two of us asked if we could pray for her and her son. She agreed, and we did.

We prayed that God would give her the courage to make it through. We prayed that God would keep her son protected and in his presence. We prayed that God would turn this burden into a blessing. We prayed for nearly fifteen minutes by simply praising God for his goodness and his mercy.

I'm not sure to this day what happened to her son, but I still remember her saying to me the next time I saw her how moved she was by our prayers. She thanked me from the bottom of her heart and simply said, "That really helped me. Thank you!"

I replied, "Not as much as it helped me!" I said that because it was at that moment that I realized I had not only served the Lord, I had met him in the vulnerability of that woman.

You see, when God sends someone to your group who needs help and if you respond, the blessing is really mutual because you've also experienced a moment in your ministry that was real, authentic, and ordained by God. But even better than that — you've experienced the power of Jesus Christ working through you, and you faithfully gave it to another. You have become a vessel for God and have had the blessing of seeing a miracle happen in your midst.

Isn't that what faith is all about?

## Time For Reflection

1. Describe any teams you've been part of in your life. What were the most valuable lessons learned?

2. What would an ideal small group look like for you?

3. Tell the story of a time in your life that another Christian helped you when you were in need?

4. How often do you pray for other people in your church? Do you do this alone? How does it make you feel?

5. What prevents most people from being part of a fellowship inside of the church? Is this happening in your church? What can be done to change it?

# Chapter Four

# Our God-Given *Giftedness*

*Now there are varieties of gifts, but the same Spirit;
and there are varieties of services, but the same
Lord; and there are varieties of activities, but it is
the same God who activates all of them in
everyone. To each is given the manifestation of the
Spirit for the common good. To one is given
through the Spirit the utterance of wisdom, and to
another the utterance of knowledge according to
the same Spirit, to another faith by the same Spirit,
to another gifts of healing by the one Spirit, to
another the working of miracles, to another
prophecy, to another the discernment of spirits, to
another various kinds of tongues, to another the
interpretation of tongues. All these are activated
by one and the same Spirit, who allots to each one
individually just as the Spirit chooses.*
— 1 Corinthians 12:4-11

A good friend of mine has a very interesting hobby. He collects tools. If you were to walk into his garage you'd be amazed at how big his collection has grown throughout the years. In his four-car garage he has plenty of saws and hammers, air compressors and hydraulic lifts, wrenches and screwdrivers, power tools and garden tools of all sizes.

Way off in the corner of his garage, he has tools that are never used. In fact, no one is allowed to even touch them. They just sit there year after year, as shiny as the day he bought them. Without a scratch and in perfect condition, they are never used. My friend likes to say that those are his show pieces. Tools that are too pretty to get dirty. (Hey, we all have our quirks!)

Whenever I visit his garage I can't help but think about what happens when the doors of the garage close at night. I imagine that the active tools tell wonderful stories of how they trimmed tall bushes, or fixed a leaky pipe, or lifted a 5,000-pound truck into the air. Some like to boast about how strong they are.

I'm sure in the world of tools there are many stories to tell and many bragging rights to be had. Then I began thinking about those *other* tools. The ones that are not doing what they were made to do. The ones considered "too pretty to get dirty." There they sit, year after year, and sadly without even a single story to tell.

That kind of reminds me of the church in some ways. In it God has collected people from around the world. We are made to be his tools for a broken world. We consist of poor people and rich people, black people and white people, males and females. Not only has he gathered us together, but he has designed each one of us the same way a craftsman designs his own tools — and that is with the very special ability to carry out certain tasks within the mission of the church. This ability is called a gift and every gift is needed for the church to be the healthy body of Christ that God designed us to be.

First Corinthians 12:4-11 says specifically that some have the gift of wisdom, some of knowledge, some have a very strong faith in the Lord, and some the ability to do healings. We also know that some Christians have the gift of teaching, preaching, playing an instrument, or singing music. Some have patience, artistic design, or the heart to do missionary work in the world. Whatever it may be, the Lord designs us all with unique gifts that become tools for God to reach out to the world with the gospel message of Jesus Christ.

In fact, it says in Ephesians 2:10: "For we are what he has made us, created in Christ Jesus for good works, which God prepared beforehand to be our way of life." We are all divinely designed and uniquely created to do good works in the name of Jesus Christ.

Have you ever noticed that not everyone uses the gifts that God gives them to carry out the church's mission? Many people are just like those tools that never get used and who have no exciting God stories of their own. Year after year they just sit around taking up space in the pews, but not actively utilizing their God-given gifts. Sure, they're shiny and beautiful, but if they're not doing what God created them to do; of what use are they to the mission of the church?

Let none of us forget that God has called all of his people to service through his grace. That means you! So often we take God and his word for granted and seek the easy road. Dietrich Bonhoeffer, recognizing this tendency in some, referred to this slothful behavior as those who celebrate "cheap grace." He wrote:

> Cheap grace is the preaching of forgiveness without requiring repentance, baptism without church discipline, Communion without confession, absolution without personal confession. Cheap grace is grace without discipleship, grace without the cross, grace without Jesus Christ, living and incarnate.
>
> Costly grace is the treasure hidden in the field; for the sake of it a man will gladly go and sell all that he has. It is the pearl of great price to buy which the merchant will sell all his goods. It is the kingly rule of Christ, for whose sake a man will pluck out the eye which causes him to stumble; it is the call of Jesus Christ at which the disciple leaves his nets and follows him.[7]

All around us we see violence, corruption, greed, racism, and other evil permeating the world we live in. Some of us just shake our heads and point our fingers and do nothing. Isn't that cheap grace?

It's these atrocities that stir the desires of Christians with a passionate spirituality to make changes, to seek justice, and to pursue the vision that God had for the world when he created it: a world filled with goodness, love, and peace for all. In order to be an effective ministry and the body of Christ in the world, we need every single Christian in the church to discover and use the gifts with which God has already blessed him or her. This most definitely includes you!

**The True Body Of Christ**

Centuries ago, Saint Paul got word that the church in Corinth was having some growing pains. There were factions and scandals, debates, dissenters, and heretics, and those who were most likely indifferent to it all. Not unlike some of our churches today! But what really grabbed Paul's attention were the few who believed that their gifts were too insignificant to matter. Wanting them to see things differently, he wrote

> *Indeed, the body does not consist of one member but of many. If the foot would say, "Because I am not a hand, I do not belong to the body," that would not make it any less a part of the body. And if the ear would say, "Because I am not an eye, I do not belong to the body," that would not make it any less a part of the body. If the whole body were an eye, where would the hearing be? If the whole body were hearing, where would the sense of smell be? But as it is, God arranged the members in the body, each one of them, as he chose.*
>
> — 1 Corinthians 12:14-18

Brilliantly, Saint Paul compares the church to the human body pointing out that it needs every one of us to be healthy and fully functioning, just as the human body needs all of its own members. Although we are all designed differently, and some of our gifts might be more or less pronounced than others, the truth is that we all have something to offer. There's no such thing as an unimportant gift from God nor an insignificant person in the body of Christ.

Author and theologian, Charles Van Engen, agreed. He wrote:

> In the New Testament it is the **whole people of God** together who are called to be the Church. All the members are joined to grow up into maturity, to the stature of the fullness of Christ (Ephesians 4:15). Such fullness is not possible if only 10 percent or fewer exercise their place and calling. Fullness will be found when the other 90% join in ministry.[8]

The church I serve today can attest to that fact. Over fifty years ago, a pastor in a nearby church had the idea and vision of building a mission start church in a little seaside resort town called Lavallette, New Jersey. He knew that if he was going to make this vision a reality he would have to find people who had the gifts to make it possible. Together with a group of about twelve people he started asking the most basic question, "What would it take to build a church?"

Over many nights, this small group met and started putting the pieces of the puzzle together. Before they knew it there were many great ideas and a lot of excitement about what could be. They imagined reaching families who vacationed there in the summer, and year-round residents who were without a church home. Before long, they had a long list of possibilities. But there was still one big hurdle to overcome: Where would they find the people to do the work and where would they find the resources?

To the pastor's surprise, each one of those twelve people agreed to offer whatever they could to make the dream come true. It was a start. One man said, "I'm pretty good with building furniture. Why don't you let me build an altar and a few chairs?"

Another man said, "I know the superintendent at the elementary school. Why don't I go there and see if they'll let us use the gym until we can find property of our own?"

One of the women said, "I can gather a bunch of people together and we can go from door to door letting everyone in town know about what we're up to. We can invite everyone to our first worship service."

Another woman offered to play the piano, a few promised to sing, and some even pledged money to pay the new minister.

A few years after that initial meeting, Faith Lutheran Church of Lavallette was erected. Today, it sits thirteen houses from the Atlantic Ocean, on property that was donated by a very generous man, and continues to be a very visible ministry in town. We try never to forget that all of this happened because every person contributed something. It's true that everyone matters in the body of Christ.

You see, great ministry happens when everyone makes a contribution. It happens when people see the need and meet it by offering a gift that God has first given to them. What becomes very obvious when gifts are being used to bless the Lord is that every single person matters and every single gift they possess is needed. I don't mean this in some abstract theological sense, but in a very practical way.

Go ahead and see for yourself! Start using your gifts and you will find a deeper sense of ownership and sense of investment like you've never felt before. Church will no longer be a place where you only come on Sunday, it will become a thread that weaves itself into your life so securely that everything else will pale in comparison. You might even begin to feel some passion for the ministry. Imagine that!

That is the vision that God has for every Christian and for every church — that it be filled with faithful people who share all things for the advancement of God's kingdom here on earth. God's vision is that all of us take ownership of the ministry he calls us to and that we invest our best to make the gospel known to all.

# Time For Reflection

1. Name three gifts that you believe are your God-given gifts and could impact your ministry greatly if you used them to build up the kingdom of earth. If you are already using your gifts, what fruits have you seen from your labor? (Examples might include: new members have joined the church, new food pantry is feeding the poor, a grief ministry was started because of you, and so on.)

2. Do you believe that most Christians use their gifts to serve God? Why or why not?

3. Have you ever been surprised to find out that you had more talent than you first expected? If so, please describe.

4. What do you think of the church being the body of Christ? What part of the body would you be?

5. Describe ways to show God how thankful you are for the gifts you possess.

## Chapter Five

# Good Stewardship:
# Giving Our Best

*For we brought nothing into the world, and we
can take nothing out of it.*
— 1 Timothy 6:7 (NIV)

Growing up in a Lutheran church, we always had a place
in the worship service immediately following the offering
where we all said in unison, "We offer with joy and thanksgiving what you have first given us — ourselves, our time,
and our possessions, signs of your gracious love. Receive them
for the sake of him who offered himself for us, Jesus Christ
our Lord. Amen." I'm not sure if all of us who recited these
words on Sunday mornings actually understood the meaning
of what was being said, but we were acknowledging that everything we have is not our own.

Imagine that for a moment! Nothing that we have is ours,
not even our bodies. Everything belongs to God.

Before we can fully understand what giving is all about
we must first understand what ownership means. So often in
our culture and world that we live in, we are led to believe
that certain things are owned by us. We might say that we
own a home, a car, a boat, or even something as simple as a
loaf of bread. They are things that we have purchased with
the money we have earned, or have been given, and we possess them for a period of time.

But do we really own these things? Legally speaking, we
do. In fact, laws and regulations are in place to acknowledge

that we are the sole proprietors of our possessions. Sometimes we keep receipts to prove a form of payment has been made even on the smaller items that are purchased. We are even categorized into a higher or lesser social status by what we own or do not own.

According to scripture we own nothing. We are reminded of this painful reality in Psalm 24:1: "The earth is the Lord's and all that is in it, the world, and those who live in it." What we acknowledge as we grow in Christ is that God is the true owner of the entire world and all that is in it: ourselves, our time, and our possessions, all of which are signs of God's gracious love. For some that can be a very sobering and humbling discovery that can take a lifelong journey to understand.

Rather, the church often refers to Christians as *stewards*. From steward we get the word "stewardship," which simply means that the steward manages property on behalf of another. Although the word stewardship isn't used in the vernacular as often as it once was, it implies great responsibility. Stewards are expected to manage property and possessions wisely and for a specific period of time. Upon returning the property the steward gives an accounting to the owner of how it was used.

This is true for us today and will be true for us on the last day; that everything we have been given in our lives is ours to hold but not to own. One day, we, too, will give God an accounting of how these possessions were managed.

Needless to say this is not always easy to digest. Nor does it make everyone very excited. On the one hand we're told by society that we are the sole proprietors of it all. At the same time, the Bible and the church tell us that we are only stewards. This means that as Christians we all live with a constant tension of having our feet in two kingdoms and there really is no easy resolution. In fact, even Jesus warned, "No one can serve two masters; for a slave will either hate the one and love the other, or be devoted to the one and despise the other. You cannot serve God and wealth" (Matthew 6:24). So what do we do?

Spiritual maturity, it seems to me, comes at the moment we can claim and assume our true identity as steward and not as owner. It comes when we stop seeking security in the idols of possessions or wealth and humble ourselves to believe that true security can only come when we are in the good graces of our Father in heaven. Spiritual maturity arrives when we can honestly admit that everything in the entire world including ourselves belongs to God. It's not easy to do, and is not without its consequences, but unless as Christians we can first acknowledge the truth about our purpose in life, there will always be a disconnect between what we say we believe and what happens in our hearts.

### Giving Our Best

In her book, *God Is No Fool*, poet and author, Lois Cheney, tells a story about one man's failure to give God anything other than his second best. She writes:

> *Once, there was a man who said, "If I had some extra money, I'd give it to God, but I have just enough money to support myself and my family."*
>
> *And the same man said, "If I had a talent I'd give it to God, but I have no lovely voice; I have no special skill; I've never been able to lead a group; I can't think cleverly or quickly, the way I would like to."*
>
> *Well, God heard the man and was touched, and although it was unlike him, God gave that man money, time, and a glorious talent.*
>
> *And then God waited, and waited, and waited, but the man never did the things he said he was going to do. And then after a while, God shrugged*

63

*His shoulders, and He took all of those things right*
*back from the man — the money, the time, and the*
*glorious talent.*

*Well, after a while the man sighed and said,*
*"If I only had some of that money back, I'd give it*
*to God. If only I had some of that time, I'd give it*
*to God. If I could rediscover that glorious talent,*
*I'd give it all to God."*

*And God said, "Oh, shut up!"*[9]

I can't tell you how many people come up to me in church on Sunday mornings and tell me that if they win the lottery, or strike it big one day they're going to do *this* or *that* for our ministry. There's always this thought in the minds of many Christians that if only there is an excess and/or it is safe to give to the church then they just might reach into their pockets and give back to God with extravagance.

I find that like the man in Lois Cheney's story all it ever leads to is lip service. Think about it for a moment. The odds of winning the lottery in one's lifetime is more than a million to one. This means that for many people the odds of ever becoming good stewards of God's resources is about the same.

Christians who see themselves as stewards take a different approach. They've come to realize that giving is part of the responsibility that comes with God's calling to manage his belongings. Stewards realize that one cannot manage God's property and possessions wisely if one does not follow the owners' requests, which is to give back some of the earnings fairly.

How does one give fairly? Especially when living in a society where many have more than most of the world. The church has inherited from ancient Israel the law code of the tithe (which means "tenth"). God, the owner of all things, asks that we give back at least a tenth of what we manage. That's a 90% return on all that we hold. That's not bad when you consider where interest rates and stock markets have taken us in recent years.

Craig L. Nessan wrote:

> *The reason to consider the tithe is for the sake of organizing an assault on one's idolatry of money. If God is indeed the owner of all that has been apportioned to me, then my only proper response is thanksgiving and gratitude for all God has provided. This certainly includes my time and talents but also my financial resources. To God belongs not just 10% but the entire 100% of what I have. In order to begin to loosen the vice grip that money has on our lives, however, one chooses to commit to the tithe as a symbol of intent. It is as if someone says, "I intend to direct my loyalty and pledge my allegiance to God above all things. As a token of this commitment, I offer a tithe of my income to the work of the kingdom."* [10]

We all know that nothing competes for our allegiance more than money, and what we do with it says a lot about what we value and idol. In fact, scripture says, "For where your treasure is, there your heart will be also" (Luke 12:34). For Christians, our treasure is the kingdom of heaven and tithing reminds us who we must first serve — the maker of all things. We strive to serve him by becoming as generous as he has been to us.

In fact, even Dietrich Bonhoeffer made the same point when he said,

> *Earthly goods are given to be used, not to be collected. In the wilderness God gave Israel the manna every day, and they had no need to worry about food and drink. Indeed, if they kept any of the manna over until the next day, it went bad. In*

*the same way, the disciple must receive his portion from God every day. If he stores it up as a permanent possession, he spoils not only the gift, but himself as well, for he sets his heart on accumulated wealth, and makes it a barrier between himself and God. Where our treasure is, there is our trust, our security, our consolation and our God. Hoarding is idolatry!*[11]

Now I'll be the first to admit that stewardship is one of the most challenging spiritual exercises of our faith, but it's also one of the most rewarding. I remember years ago seeing firsthand how the generosity of Christians can touch the lives of so many. We were collecting Christmas toys and clothing for an underprivileged family in our area. For weeks we encouraged the congregation to be generous and extravagant in their purchases.

On Christmas Eve of that year, along with one of the deacons in our church, I delivered the many bags of toys, clothing, and gift certificates to the house. When the mother answered the door she was seemingly surprised to see us and cautiously invited us in. It was fairly obvious, upon a quick look around, that this family was struggling financially, but what broke my heart were the four tiny packages under the tree that were carefully wrapped in the Sunday comics — two with the name of "Jessica" and the other two with the name of "Brian." Evidently it was going to be a lean year for this poor family.

Without causing embarrassment, we said to the mother as the children listened, "Here are the packages you ordered!" The mother's eyes began to well up as she gave us a hug to show her appreciation. Then we said before we left, "And here is a gift from us," as we handed her a Bible.

To this day I'm not sure how their Christmas turned out or if they were moved enough to praise God for his goodness, but I can tell you that it moved me. It made me realize first-hand how one's generosity and kindness expresses God's love to the world. It inspired me to want to share that care and compassion with others and I have found that striving to tithe is the best way.

In the Evangelical Lutheran Church of America (ELCA), we are encouraged to tithe so that we, as a church-wide body, can support ministries throughout the world. I am proud to say that the ELCA has ministries in Africa, the Middle East, Asia, South America, the US, and elsewhere, building new churches, homes, schools, hospitals, and clinics for the poor and most vulnerable of the world. This is only possible because of the many generous people who see it as their mission in life to give back to the one who first blessed them. It's how they worship our Lord Jesus Christ.

I understand that not everyone is in a position financially to give 10% of their income. Some of us are busy raising families, or living on very tight budgets, or we're between jobs. Rather than getting caught up with numbers I think it's more important that we focus on our attitude toward giving rather than how much we actually give. Each time we think about giving back to God we should ask, "Does this show God my gratitude? Does my offering praise God? Am I giving God my best?"

A few years ago, I remember talking about the topic of stewardship with the local pastors who belonged to our clergy cluster. Everyone could identify two or three people in their congregations that were outstanding in the generosity and compassion they had toward the poor.

One of the pastors who belonged to the non-denominational church in the area told of a new member who had recently joined his church. The new member wasn't a very wealthy man but was eager to get involved and show God his gratitude by serving. One Sunday after the worship service, the pastor got up and reminded the congregation of their needed mission support. They were hoping to send a few people to South America so that they could help build a new church.

The pastor said that he later found plenty of money in the offering plate to make the trip feasible. He thanked God for the blessing and for the generosity of the people in the church. What surprised and impressed him the most was a rolled up piece of paper with the words "myself" written on it and signed by the new member. Although the man could not give as much money as most people in his congregation, he had the right attitude toward giving and he was still able to give his best.

In so many ways, that is the expectation we should have for ourselves. We might not all be financially gifted but we all have something to give back to God and to the world and that is ourselves. Never forget who you are, and more importantly, never forget *whose* you are. You are God's own and a beloved steward.

### It All Begins With You

I am going to guess that out of all the chapters in this book this one will remain unread by the majority of people. By now some readers are already onto the conclusion of the book and I suspect all others who've kept reading this far might be feeling a bit uncomfortable. I'll be the first to admit that reading this chapter would have made me feel uncomfortable years ago, as well. It's so easy to just ignore this part of our spirituality and think to ourselves, "I'd rather not deal with the whole idea of giving right now. I'm happy just doing what I've been doing."

But are you *really* happy? I mean, can anyone who knows and loves the Lord, and who has been filled with his Spirit, really be happy when we haven't fully considered his words? Can we really be happy deep down in our spirits when we've cut corners and haven't completely opened ourselves up to what Jesus Christ has for us? I don't think so. I am seeking a passionate and sincere spirituality and have come to the conclusion that giving back to God has to be a central part of my faith life. Wouldn't you agree for yourself?

When I was a child, a visiting pastor came to our congregation and told us that since we are managers of God's resources, on the last day all of us would stand before God and give an accounting of how we lived our lives. As a child that intrigued me to some degree and has always left me wanting to follow Jesus ever more deeply so that I can discover all that he has in store for me. I'm sure, if he has touched your life you'd want to do the same.

Let me just tell you that in the last fifteen years the process of discovering God's will about giving has been anything but painful or burdensome. In fact, in many ways it has been deeply enlightening and liberating. No longer do I feel that money has complete control over my life or my decision making. At the same time, I've learned more about what it means to trust God and celebrate his grace than ever before.

This is true because I believe the good stewardship of one's resources is equal to the measure of one's spiritual health. And giving back to God carries with it blessings that can't be compared to anything else. It is one of the greatest forms of worship we can do.

I could go on and on about the benefits of giving and how it increases our awareness of the working of the Spirit, but suffice it to say that if you are serious about deepening your walk with Christ, and growing spiritually passionate, there is no other way to experience spiritual growth in this area than by simply doing it yourself. Go ahead and give with extravagance and become, through time, a better steward of what God first gave you. I can promise you that you'll never regret a single moment if it's done in the name of the Lord.

It all begins with you!

## Time For Reflection

1.  Why is talking about money such a sensitive subject for some Christians? How does it make you feel to talk about money?

2.  Describe a time when you were generous. How did it make you feel and what was the outcome of your efforts?

3.  Describe the role of a manager. What makes her responsible and trustworthy? What makes her negligent in her duties?

4.  If it's true that we are stewards of God's resources would you hire someone like yourself to manage your own resources? In other words, does your giving represent what a good steward looks like?

5.  How can you become a better steward?

# Conclusion

Your relationship with the Lord shouldn't be boring and unsatisfying. That's not what you want and it's definitely not what God wants for you. Spirituality is a beautiful gift from the Lord that should, and can, constantly amaze us, inspire us, leave us in awe, and fill us with passion. It is my great hope that in the coming days, months, and years as you begin to cultivate your faith life that you also experience the joy in meeting Jesus Christ anew again and again on the pathways of your life.

In many churches throughout the world this reality is already happening in the hearts of God's people. I'm being told that revivals are taking place, new churches are being erected, and newfound believers are committing themselves to serving Jesus Christ in all that they do. For the first time in a long time the church is once again being filled with true believers like you. Praise be to God!

I suppose in some ways this shouldn't surprise any of us. Just look around and you can see that there is a deep hunger for spiritual connectedness in our increasingly secular and "godless" society. You and I are not unique in wanting to put God at the center of our lives and discovering what our true and meaningful purpose is in life. Millions of other people are also seeking that same fulfillment and wanting the same hope that the Lord will recognize them on the day of judgment. That's why I pray that every reader of this book comes to find the peace that I myself have found in writing it.

Begin anew by telling your story of God's amazing grace to all who will listen. Hear it yourself for the first time. Embrace what God has done for you and live as if nothing else is as meaningful in this world. Take time to realize that in the eyes of God you matter greatly. Then come to the house of the Lord and celebrate this extravagant love week after week. Let the passion you have for God come alive!

As I have tried to express in the writing of this book, passionate spirituality requires courage. In fact, to be a faithful Christian in the world we are living in means that we must first be willing to walk in a different direction than most people. We walk in the footsteps of Christ. In order to keep steady on the path ahead we must always be willing to put fear behind us.

As you begin this new and exciting adventure take time each day to remind yourself that you're not alone on your journey. The Lord will constantly look down on you and smile as he sees you being transformed from what you once were to what he'd have you become. From this point forward you will never be the same. So brace yourself!

I want to encourage you from time to time to go back to each chapter and especially review the "Time For Reflection" questions provided in this book. They're meant to help you see progress in your development and also to help you identify specific areas that might need more attention. Keep this book handy as an ongoing resource that can help remind you of who you are and who you are becoming.

Although it isn't required, some might find it most helpful to read this book together with a group. The constant interaction between other Christians will broaden your understanding of the content included in this book and will at times challenge you to consider new things about yourself, the world, and most importantly God.

Many blessings to you from this point onward. It's my prayer that the Holy Spirit will blow through you with gentleness and joy.

I'd appreciate hearing from you. You can contact me via the internet at jtcollins56@hotmail.com. Let me hear what God is doing in your life.

Much peace.

— John T. Collins

# Endnotes

1. "Cheap grace" was first referenced by Dietrich Bonhoeffer. It suggests faith without obedience to the teachings of Jesus Christ. In other words, there is no challenge or command to turn away from sin. One hears the words of absolution (or God's forgiveness) and yet continues on the same path.

2. This was an article given to me by a friend and was without proper bibliographical data. I wanted to include it in this book because of its relevancy to the issue of God's grace.

3. Names, gender, and places have been changed to protect the confidentiality of those who have shared their pain and struggle with me through the years.

4. Piper, John, *The Legacy of Sovereign Joy: God's Triumphant Grace in the Lives of Augustine, Luther, and Calvin* (Wheaton, Illinois: Crossway Books, 2000), p. 90.

5. Fryer, Kelly A., *Reclaiming the "C" Word: Daring to be Church Again* (Minneapolis: Augsburg Fortress, 2006), p. 41.

6. Bonhoeffer, Dietrich, *Life Together: A Discussion of Christian Fellowship by Dietrich Bonhoeffer*, trans. John W. Doberstein (New York: Harper & Brothers, 1954), p. 30.

7. Bonhoeffer, Dietrich, *The Cost of Discipleship* (New York: Touchstone, 1995), pp. 44-45.

8. Van Engen, Charles, *God's Missionary People: Rethinking the Purpose of the Local Church* (Grand Rapids, Michigan: Baker Book House, 1991), p. 151.

9. Cheney, Lois, *God Is No Fool* (Nashville: Abingdon Press, 1969), p. 155.

10. Nessan, Craig L., *Beyond Maintenance to Mission: A Theology of the Congregation* (Minneapolis: Fortress Press, 1999), p. 73. I have

been truly inspired by Craig L. Nessan. His work has not only inspired me and clarified my thinking but has influenced the direction of this chapter.

11. *Op cit*, Bonhoeffer, *The Cost of Discipleship*, p. 175.

www.ingramcontent.com/pod-product-compliance
Lightning Source LLC
Chambersburg PA
CBHW072229050426
42443CB00032B/876